YOUR FINANCIAL "PERP" WALK

Millennial Friendly Personal Finance
1st Edition

by

Prester Khan

DORRANCE
PUBLISHING CO
EST 1920
PITTSBURGH, PENNSYLVANIA 15238

Dorrance Publishing Co
585 Alpha Drive
Pittsburgh, PA 15238
Visit our website at *www.dorrancebookstore.com*

ISBN: 978-1-6470-2265-5
eISBN: 978-1-6470-2878-7

Contents

Introduction   v

Your Financial PERP Walk   1

Cause   3

Finance Is a Discipline   5

Investment   9

Build It, and Pass It On   15

Financial Commandments   17

How to Pass It On   19

Conclusion   21

Epilogue   23

Abbreviations   25

INTRODUCTION

This blueprint is written in the style of being direct and to the point. I'm not here to create the next Warren Buffet, nor am I auditioning for a literary prize. I write so that you can read, understand, and execute this blueprint. This blueprint is the minimum you need to do for financial success. I'm not here to impress you with the breadth and depth of my financial knowledge. I'm here to start a grassroots movement that anyone can save and invest at a basic level and still do fine. I've distilled personal finance to a basic blueprint that anyone can understand and execute. Anyone can leave a financial legacy. All that it requires is a beginning, a few principles, a little discipline, and some restraint to perpetuate itself. Therefore, this blueprint is concise.

Who am I to lecture you on personal finance? Just your average financial professional who's spent 20-plus years working for banks and financial software firms analyzing and quantifying their risks for financial instruments, interest rate derivatives, and currency derivatives. I also hold undergraduate and graduate degrees. Should you need more credentials and details, please send a cup for urinalysis and a self-addressed, postage paid packet for the results. Anyways, this is not a lecture, but a blueprint for personal finance success. As such, most of this you can do, but there are a couple of areas that require outside expertise and you coming up to speed. You will need legal expertise for setting up your bequests to your heirs, and you may need some financial expertise on diversification and retirement planning. I'm providing the 80 percent to get you most of the way by yourself and letting you know the remaining 20 percent you need to outsource to get you the rest of the way.

I have littered this blueprint with anagrams. There are two reasons for this, and the first reason is fake. First, it should help maintain demand for alphabet soup. More seriously, these anagrams help make the principles described easier to remember. They are done in the style of typical text messaging abbreviations and Twitter hashtags. Half of any discipline is remembering to do it; and the execution half of personal finance in most cases is easy. Hopefully, they will catch on, and personal finance groups will spontaneously form using these anagrams in their communications.

Your Financial PERP Walk

What will your "Financial PERP" walk be like? Perp is a double entendre and abbreviation. Perp walk in legal lingo refers to a public arrest or public detention of a civilian with much fanfare and publicity for a crime. Perp is short for perpetrator, usually of a crime. Financially, PERP is short for perpetuity. A perpetuity is a financial instrument that pays interest or dividends in perpetuity, or forever. I believe it to be the ultimate financial goal to which everyone should aspire. I refer to the "Financial PERP" walk as entering your retirement until you pass away. Do you have any retirement savings? Or will you be relying upon social security along with the resources of your family and friends?

Will it be like going to jail? Or will it be like an ongoing parade in your celebration?

The great thing about finance is that you get partial credit no matter how short you fall of this goal so long as you pass it on. And passing on a little bit of savings can yield large advantages to your descendants with compounding over long periods of time and your descendants' additional savings and investment; it's called TOYS or #TOYS, or time is on your side. True wealth is not the accumulation of stuff; it is the acquisition of time.

Everyone does their financial PERP walk; or walks their financial green mile. So, will your green mile be mired in financial distress affecting family and friends alike? Will it be like that long walk from death row to the electric chair? Or will you have a comfortable retirement with future generations singing your praises when you pass? This is my blueprint for making your own "Financial PERP" walk a perennial Superbowl touchdown dance.

Cause

I believe a financial perpetuity to be a worthy cause for a few reasons. It allows people to reap the benefits of capitalism for both themselves and generations to come. This is a great benefit when economies go bad and job opportunities are scarce or having to weather health emergencies and natural disasters. You get to help future generations that you will never meet, and they get to be thankful for prior generations they may have never known of otherwise. By the way, a trust for your perpetuity is an excellent way to keep up and maintain your ancestry tree. Just think, you can store pictures, videos, and all kinds of memorabilia in your trust. It can be more than just your financial history, but a much more comprehensive history of your ancestry. You can now establish that thread through history of your antecedents and your descendants. More important than the perpetuity itself are the virtues, discipline, and organizational skills required to build the perpetuity itself. Modesty, temperance, and preparation are but a few of these.

Finally, here is the number one cause: you win as long as you play, no matter what. So many people criticize youth sports for giving teams a trophy when they didn't win anything or otherwise called a "participation trophy." Now, here we have a cause that pays money as long as you participate at all and pays you more if you participate more. And almost everyone is on the sidelines! It's like they have taken a vow of poverty! I'm certain that politicians have taken a vow of poverty for their constituencies for several generations with their profligate spending!

I guess the real reason I'm here is to ask aloud the questions that people don't realize they are answering with inaction. Actually, I am not here to ask the questions aloud, I am here to proclaim the answers aloud with emphasis.

These are the exclamations for a successful financial PERP walk:

1) SAY YES TO SAVINGS!
2) SAY YES TO INVESTMENT!
3) SAY YES TO DIVIDEND REINVESTMENT
4) SAY YES...TO YOUR FINANCIAL PERP WALK!!!

Finance Is a Discipline

Personal finance is a discipline when it comes to reaching financial goals. There are all kinds of investment choices from the most basic to the most esoteric. This blueprint does not require you to learn or even know all or even most of these to reach your goals. In finance, doing the basics well will set you up just fine.

Discipline is just creating a good habit. And these are the habits that you need to make lifelong and pass on to your heirs. There are a few basic disciplines of finance that are timeless. So DBD (don't be dumb), MFD (master financial discipline).

So, what is the first basic discipline of finance? The first basic discipline of finance is saving. Save early, and save often. Don't worry; I'll expound with more specific advice than that.

Saving early is much more important than later, and I would say critical to creating your own perpetuity. To avoid the excuse of "I can't afford to save," embedded in the discipline of saving is the practice of not over committing financially. Saving should start as early as possible to teach the habit but usually does not begin in earnest until one gets that first job. When you enter the permanent workforce, you should save 20 percent of your income: 10 percent is for emergency savings; and 10 percent is for retirement investments or half-n-half (HNH).

Retirement investments should generally be in a protected investment vehicle like 401k, IRA, Roth IRA, etc. These accounts provide bankruptcy protection for your retirement savings. Too often, people save in these accounts and then raid them when they get into financial distress. That is a big no-no! Withdrawing the funds can cause penalties. Borrowing against these accounts negates the tax deferral benefit of a regular 401k and IRA because you have to pay back the loan with after tax dollars. Don't be fooled with a low interest rate when tax rates are so much higher. By the way, after you pay back the loan, those funds will be taxed again when you withdraw them for retirement. Even if you pay back the loan with pre-tax current contributions, you will have given up years of dividends and price appreciation plus additional contributions to your account that are now paying back the loan. To sum up, never ever withdraw funds or borrow against retirement accounts before retirement.

Even when you have a lot saved and may not need to save more, I recommend saving 5-10 percent anyways to keep the habit as a part of your life and prevent the possibility of spending too much.

Emergency savings should be in a separate bank account. Once your emergency savings reach $100k, you can use it for capital outlays like a down payment on a house and draw down as much as necessary. For other capital outlays, like cars, don't draw down below $50k. Alternatively, you can create a taxable investment account and fund it without going below $50k. Once the emergency savings has been drawn down, continue to replenish it until it gets back to $100k. Then, rinse and repeat (RNR). Please note that all 20% of savings should be going to investment once emergency savings are fully funded.

Again, EFD (Enforce Financial Discipline). Legitimate drawings of emergency reserves are for health issues and income replacement when there is a job loss. You should especially use emergency savings for high deductibles to lower insurance premiums everywhere possible, also use for co-pays. Again, RNR.

Now you know to save and how much to save and to replenish savings, but you don't know how to save. There is a reason that saving is the first priority in your personal budget. In order to save, you have to make sure your expenditures don't prevent you from saving. You have to take into account all your expected expenditures with some allowance to create an environment that allows you to save. This is the discipline of not over committing financially. DBD, EFD is ESD (enforcing financial discipline is enforcing spending discipline). Often people commit too much financially to assets, which prevent them from saving, and it is not a good practice to borrow to save. So, you need to budget, and the first item in the budget is saving. Then, you need to itemize the other expected expenses and see what you can or need to reduce. The more detail and precision, the better. All this needs to happen before you get a place to stay and decide on transportation. Don't forget to budget for insurance like health, disability, car, etc. This is particularly important for kids or grads getting their first job, as too often they end up starting off in the hole, if they haven't already dug one with student loans and credit cards. Too often, people climb out of the hole only to repeat the process instead of learning from it and getting on the path to saving. DBD, LFD (learn financial discipline), and EFD. You will need to adjust your budget several times probably before you know what you can truly afford. Once you have your plan, follow it, and account for everything you spend. That means keeping all your receipts, tallying them up, and seeing if you stay within your budget. Budgeting usually cries out for some sort of spreadsheet to plan. So create a spreadsheet or get a program or app. Remember that your budget is maximum spending; it is not like a government budget or required spending. You want to spend less than your budget. Saving is a discipline that requires lower spending to fund. Don't panic if you have a hard time meeting your goals early on and have small variances. Review your receipts against your plan. Think of everything that you can do to get within your plan. If those changes are doable, then make those changes and do it. If you conclude that it is just not plausible to find the savings to stay within your plan, you should re-review your budget to make your goals more realistic and maybe save 10 percent. This should not be upsetting if you are relatively new or have had a major life change. Make the new budget and stick to it. RNR (rinse and repeat).

So try to find the cheapest way to do everything you do in living. Use coupons, take advantage of specials, buy small iced tea if refills are free, avoid finance charges and make living economically a way of life. This will not only help you with saving money, but also make you a better judge of the economy and investments and a much better consumer. You can also find more economical entertainment of all kinds like books and hobbies. You might even volunteer for charity work. You might even take on some extra work on the side if you have time. If you're not spending time making money, you're spending time spending money. So STMM, not STSM.

So far, I haven't specified what your target retirement savings should be for retirement. I'm not sure if I should, but I will because you need to know. To determine the size of your retirement perpetuity, take the annual income you will need to live on in retirement and divide that by the dividend yield of the market or S&P 500. If I need an annual income of $100,000 in retirement and the dividend yield of the S&P 500 is 2.5 percent, I need to save $100,000 / .025 = $4,000,000. If you need to do a freak out scream now, go ahead, but do a silent scream if you're in public. Take a deep breath while I do some splainin. Remember this amount gets you a perpetuity (forever) of $100,000 annually. This doesn't account for Social Security or pension payments. That can bring it down to $2,000,000 if you get $50,000 from SS or a pension. Additionally, living below your means and being frugal will bring down the annual income you require in retirement. Finally, you get partial credit in this game as I mentioned before. Aiming for the higher number is a worthy goal, but don't let it discourage or deter you; getting a quarter or even half way there should allow for a decent retirement and still allow for a sizable bequest to your heirs. I don't think you will really know how much you need for retirement until you are almost retired. I think it is far more important to stress the discipline of saving, to save regularly, and to pass that knowledge to your children. For if you pass that knowledge to your children and fail to leave them an estate, you will have still succeeded.

INVESTMENT

The sooner you start saving and saving regularly, the better off you will be. I don't believe you should be more aggressive in your investing style if you were smart enough to save early.

There is no point in risking your savings, which could cause you to have to start all over. And it is not a good practice to scare some youngster or anyone out of the market altogether.

What asset class should you invest in? By far, the answer is the stock market when it comes to ordinary individuals. Bonds, CDs, savings accounts, and money market accounts don't even beat inflation over the long haul. Real estate requires a lot of capital and risk as do other asset classes.

When it comes to risk tolerance, a good investment plan is key. The ingredients to a good investment plan are performance, income, diversification and liquidity. This can be a custom plan from a financial planner or the mass market plan. Financial planners will usually have you fill out a questionnaire to determine your risk tolerance. This is a bad practice because you are answering questions on numbers without a context. Your mood or whim will determine your answers, not your confidence in an investment plan. Therefore, I recommend the mass market plan (MMP).

MMP is investing in a market benchmark, either through a low cost fund or an exchange traded fund (ETF). These funds provide market exposure, diversification, liquidity and may provide dividend reinvestment. They are economical in that they cost 10-15 basis points or less; 10 basis points is 1/10th of 1 percent. They also provide performance; 90-95 percent of actively managed funds fail to beat market indexes over long periods of time, usually 15 years or more. That means if you buy a market index fund, you'll likely beat

90 percent of actively managed funds over the long run. Think about that. Do you really want to bet on a fund manager when there is only a 5-10 percent chance of beating the market? Not only are the underlying stock shares highly liquid, but the fund shares are usually highly liquid as they are large funds. This is the ultimate set it and forget it (SIFI or #SIFI) investment strategy. There is one last note on diversification for market funds or ETFs. They do not protect against market risk. Since the market has consistently returned 7-10 percent over the long term, this strategy is appropriate for investment horizons of at least 10 years and usually better for 15 years or more. This should give you the confidence to enjoy the highs and ride out the lows. These funds will only blow up if the market blows up or it's the end of the world.

Here's more on why to invest in market funds and ETFs. Warren Buffet issued a $1 million challenge to any hedge funds that could beat the S&P 500 over 10 years. This was around 2007. A firm accepted the bet and spread the money over six hedge funds. S&P 500 beat the best performing hedge fund by more than 20 percent in total return over 10 years. The S&P 500 averaged 7.1 percent, and the six hedge funds averaged like 2 percent annually. Never mind this was around the time of the financial meltdown, where hedge funds usually outperform. The hedge funds didn't even beat the dividend rate of the S&P 500. So, MMP is the way to go. SIFI.

So where do you go to invest in a market fund or an ETF (exchange traded fund) based on a market index? These would typically come from Morningstar, SPDRs, iShares, and Vanguard fund families and fund companies. Typical tickers for the total market are IWV, VTI and VTHR. Typical tickers for the global market are VT and ACWI. Typical tickers for the S&P 500 are SPY, IVV and VOO. I recommend these due to additional advantages. They are proven companies with proven business models. Companies can't be pruned from the index because they are too large. Companies will be pruned from the index if they shrink or other better companies outgrow them. Finally, you will benefit and get a piece of the action in the case of a bailout. All of these are highly liquid, highly diversified, and cost effective investment vehicles.

You should save and invest on a monthly basis whether you participate in an employer plan or not. Again, take advantage of 401k, IRA, Roth plans for protection from bankruptcy. Especially take full advantage of your 401k if your employer offers matching funds; it's free money! (IFM! Or #IFM!)

If you come into a windfall lump sum of money, what should you do? First, set aside taxes. The following recommendations are for after tax money. If it's $150k or less, put 1/3 into emergency savings, 1/3 into retirement savings and 1/3 into spending. If it's more than $150k, put enough to get your emergency savings to $100k and split the remainder between retirement savings and spending, if the remainder is less than $100k; otherwise, spend $50k and put the remainder in your investments. When you put this money in your investments, you should dollar cost average or value average that money into the market over 12 or 24 months. This limits your price risk, so you don't put all your money in the market when it is at all time highs. However, you might reconsider if the market is at multi-year lows. Dollar cost averaging (DCA or #DCA) is investing the same dollar amount monthly, which purchases more shares at lower prices. Value averaging (VA or #VA) is percentage investing based on a market benchmark. If you have $100k to invest over 10 months and the current market benchmark is at 10k, that would be $10k a month if the market stayed flat. If the market goes to 11k, you would invest $9k. If the market goes to 5k, you would invest $50k. This causes you to invest less when the market is up and to invest more when the market is down. So, you are investing more dollars in down markets, which buys even more shares than DCA when the market is lower. You will be fully invested faster than your timeline if markets are down. You may not be fully invested within your time horizon if markets are up consistently. I recommend counting percentages against the beginning investment amount. See table below with an example of investing $10,000 over 10 months using DCA and VA.

Period	Dollar Cost Averaging (DCA)	Value Averaging (VA)	Remaining Principal DCA	Remaining Principal VA	Index	VA Percentage Adjustment	Applied VA % Adjustment
0					15000		
1	$1,000.00	$666.67	$9,000.00	$9,333.33	15500	-3.33%	6.67%
2	$1,000.00	$600.00	$8,000.00	$8,733.33	15600	-4.00%	6.00%
3	$1,000.00	$1,666.67	$7,000.00	$7,066.67	14000	6.67%	16.67%
4	$1,000.00	$2,000.00	$6,000.00	$5,066.67	13500	10.00%	20.00%
5	$1,000.00	$2,333.33	$5,000.00	$2,733.33	13000	13.33%	23.33%
6	$1,000.00	$1,333.33	$4,000.00	$1,400.00	14500	3.33%	13.33%
7	$1,000.00	$1,000.00	$3,000.00	$400.00	15000	0.00%	10.00%
8	$1,000.00	$400.00	$2,000.00	$0.00	15500	-3.33%	6.67%
9	$1,000.00	$0.00	$1,000,00	$0.00	16000	-6.67%	3.33%
10	$1,000.00	$0.00	$0.00	$0.00	16500	-10.00%	0.00%

Illustration 1: Dollar Cost Averaging (DCA) vs. Value Averaging (VA)

You should make sure you have a diversified portfolio of investments. If you have market funds or market ETFs, which I highly recommend, you are good. Although you may want to add some international investments or alternative investments for additional diversification; I am not a fan of this these days as global markets are more connected, and many large US companies are already global. Bonds may become a more attractive investment in the future and should be added when they do for diversification. There are some qualification for bonds. If yields are at all time highs like the 1980s or at least approaching double digits, you should add. If you are going to make your perpetuity goal and be able to live off the dividends, there is no need to add bonds at normal rates. If you are going to be short of your perpetuity goal and are nearing retirement, then it makes sense to add bonds. This is the best time to engage a fee only financial planner to make sure your savings will provide the income you need and will last. It may be worth checking out the holdings or top holdings of your mutual funds and ETFs to see if you have more concentration risk or less diversification than you think; this is only if you hold funds and ETFs that are not based on the market. For example, banks are part of a large number of funds so you may be more exposed to banking than you would think from fund descriptions.

If you want to invest in individual stocks, you should do so with side money keeping your market investments intact. Start with 5 percent of your investments and never more than 10 percebt of your investments. If you do invest in individual stocks, do your research. There are actually more mutual funds than there are stocks. If you do the research and have the temperament, you should do fine. If you have a large gain, reinvest half in stocks and half in your market fund or ETF after taxes.

Combined with some conservative option strategies, you can enhance your returns with minimal risk. This is advanced stuff, so you don't have to learn, and you can skip the rest of this paragraph if you like. If you learn and get comfortable with these strategies, congratulations on squeezing out a little more return on your investments. You can sell covered calls to generate additional income on stocks that have run up in value. And you can sell covered puts to recover money lost in a market downturn after the market has already dropped. You may be able to make 10 percent or more just in put premiums. You can then reinvest those premiums into the stock and be up 20 percent or more when the market fully recovers instead of just making it back to even or par.

However you decide to invest in the market, be absolutely sure to reinvest dividends (or RDIV) and put time on your side (TOYS). This is the act of compounding returns that allows your investments to grow exponentially instead of linearly. Some funds do this automatically on dividends and some investments or brokerages may allow you to set this up to work automatically. If your funds and investment accounts don't allow this, you have to do it manually and this is a commandment.

If you want to invest in other business ventures, those should be separate from your stock market holdings to limit your liability. I would be very wary of physical real estate and land investments in your protected IRAs, 401ks, etc. You are better off setting these up in your own LLC or similar vehicle.

A couple of words on annuities or any investment sold by an insurance company. Don't! They offer no compelling value.

There is a 99 percent chance you will be investing in something you don't understand and benefits the insurance company at your expense. And more likely than not, you will have to sue them even if they owe you. Remember, you surrender your money to the insurance company. With taxable and retirement investment accounts, it's your account and your money in the stock market that you can sell whenever you want.

As you grow and mature, it is natural to wade into new waters. However, you are best served by leaving your base intact and wade in with what you can afford to lose, probably 5-10 percent of your portfolio. And I am in no way telling you that you have to do it yourself. It comes down to what you do better. Do you manage your investments better, or do you manage fund managers or personal finance managers better?

So, set up your BFP (basic financial plan) and EFP (execute financial plan).

Build It, and Pass It on

We've covered saving and investment, which is building it or BFP and EFP. Now, we've come to passing it on. This is where you need a lawyer. Early on, you may just need a will. As you get closer to retirement and your nest egg has grown, you will need a comprehensive estate plan.

This is where the financial perpetuity really starts, but you need a couple of commandments to make sure you receive the benefits and make sure it endures. Your perpetuity only comes to fruition after you die. Do your heirs inherit your money lump-sum? Did you set up a trust that pays them a stipend from a certain age onward? I'm not an estate planning expert, but regardless of which way they inherit their money, determined beneficiaries and lawyers can still find ways to spend all of it even if it means busting the trust. The best way to ensure that your estate endures is to teach your children about the fundamentals of saving, restraint, personal finance and investing. Otherwise, it may just turn into a large gift to your heirs that funds some fancy trips and merchandise until it's all gone and somehow the heirs have gone into financial distress. No matter how large or small your perpetuity is, the following commandments should be attached to it:

a. NSP or never spend the principal or use it as collateral for a loan.
b. The inheritor is not absolved of the responsibility of saving their own money for their own retirement and creating their own perpetuity to add to yours. TFD.
c. The inheritor is required to teach and pass on the discipline of finance to their kids or beneficiaries. TFD.
d. Reinvest dividends or RDIV and put TOYS.

The goal is to create a perpetuity that covers all living expenses so that you don't have to work or you can still get by when you don't have a job. The job market has been bad for millennials and that could continue going forward for future generations. Also, governments have been floating the idea of a universal income program, which has to be the most obvious bribe of voters I have ever seen. The perpetuity is how you can accomplish this privately and have a much higher standard of living. I guess the ultimate goal is to be living off the compound interest or the interest on your interest. Time can benefit you and your beneficiaries, aka TOYS. Can you imagine that a bad day is when your accountant announces you are no longer living on the interest on your interest? And your wife faints at the news. That may sound far-fetched now, but it is absolutely possible in a couple of generations. This is the way a common man or woman can leave a legacy that lasts generations. Now that is a man or woman for all seasons!

FINANCIAL COMMANDMENTS

1) Save, DBD.
2) Don't over commit financially. Budget and stay within budget. DBD, EFD, and EFP.
3) Reinvest dividends or RDIV and put TOYS.
4) Don't spend perpetuity principal or DSP.
5) Pass perpetuity on or PPO.
6) Teach Financial Discipline or TFD.

How to Pass It on

The best way to pass it on legally is through a trust or possibly an LLC. In a legal sense, this may present a challenge. Recognized in case or common law is the "Rule against Perpetuities." This is intended to prevent people from controlling or managing assets from beyond the grave. It came about in England centuries ago that people could bequeath and describe how physical property (land) could be managed long after their death. This was not acceptable to the state, so they established the Rule against Perpetuities. Again, this is where your need a lawyer.

In modern day US, how does this affect us? For people with large land holdings, it may have a dramatic effect. For other financial assets, the effect may be muted. From what I understand, the federal estate taxes would not be affected much, if at all. Since property for the most part resides in the states, it is more a matter of state law. Many states have passed laws that invalidate the Rule against Perpetuities either largely or outright. Louisiana allows for perpetuities and Arizona allows for trusts that last for 500 years. This would allow the passing of financial assets (other than physical property) without issue. Again, you need a lawyer.

You can set up a Louisiana trust without having to reside in Louisiana for such a purpose; this pretty much goes for all the other states. This is a pretty sweet deal. However, you may need to consider physical land and property in your home state separately for planning purposes. And I would certainly not commingle any physical property or land with financial property to be bequeathed. Again, you need a lawyer.

Conclusion

You now have the tools for a successful financial life. If you earn 0 percent returns and have saved $20k a year for 50 years, you will have $1mm at retirement. If you earn market returns and saved $20k a year from ages 20 to 30, each $20k in savings will yield $100-$150k at retirement giving you a total of more than $1mm. If you earn market returns and saved $20k a year from ages 20 to 69, you will have $3-$5mm at retirement. So, if you're young, there is a lot to get excited about.

If you're older, this is no time to despair. You can still save and invest and leave something to your heirs. Your heirs will most likely have many years of compounding to benefit them, even with small inheritances. And you can teach them well financial discipline, which is more important for them and successive generations.

ARE YOU READY TO DO YOUR FINANCIAL PERP WALK?

EPILOGUE

The nice thing about preparing for your financial PERP walk is that you actually get an epilogue. How long it lasts depends on how well you have saved, invested, protected, and passed on to your beneficiaries.

While we acknowledge the importance of money in our everyday lives, futures and those of our beneficiaries, the size of our bank account will pale in comparison to the values and virtues we have developed and nurtured in the process of capital accumulation. Values and virtues such as modesty, thrift, temperance, chastity, patience, discipline, tenacity, faith, courage, steadfastness, charity, humility, preparedness, organizational skills, confidence, decision-making skills, etc. That is one hell of a bonus to receive and that you can pass on to your beneficiaries.

The crop has been planted and hopefully is self-sustaining. If your heirs have learned well, they will harvest the crops without digging into the seed stock. And hopefully, they will add to the seed stock for their own benefit and that of their own heirs; and so on and so forth.

There is no greater feeling than saving one's soul. Leaving a financial legacy, which is the tangible result of practicing good values and virtues would have to be next, even if it is a distant second. So when you and your heirs are asked why money never seems to be a problem, just tell them you got it through the grapevine.

ABBREVIATIONS

TOYS	→	#TOYS	→	Time is On Your Side
DBD	→	#DBD	→	Don't Be Dumb
MFD	→	#MFD	→	Master Financial Discipline
HNH	→	#HNH	→	Half-n-half
RNR	→	#RNR	→	Rinse and Repeat
EFD	→	#EFD	→	Enforce Financial Discipline
ESD	→	#ESD	→	Execute Spending discipline
LFD	→	#LFD	→	Learn Financial Discipline
STMM	→	#STMM	→	Spend Time Making Money
STSM	→	#STSP	→	Spend Time Spending Money
IFM!	→	#IFM!	→	It's Free Money!
RDIV	→	#RDIV	→	Reinvest Dividends
BFP	→	#BFP	→	Basic Financial Plan
EFP	→	#EFP	→	Execute Financial Plan
DSP	→	#DSP	→	Don't Spend Principal
NSP	→	#NSP	→	Never Spend Principal
SIFI	→	#SIFI	→	Set It and Forget It
MMP	→	#MMP	→	Mass Market Plan
DCA	→	#DCA	→	Dollar Cost Average
VA	→	#VA	→	Value Average
PPO	→	#PPO	→	Pass Perpetuity On
TFD	→	#TFD	→	Teach Financial Discipline

www.ingramcontent.com/pod-product-compliance
Lightning Source LLC
Chambersburg PA
CBHW061522180526
45171CB00001B/294